COPYRIGHT

Best Wedding Ever

AMINA GARRISON

For my loves, besties and #1 supporters
My Hilarious & Handsome Husband
Brilliant & Beautiful Daughter
Sweetest & Studly Son

contents

cheers
to happily
ever
after

As an award-winning wedding planner, I have met all of you. The "super type A" couple with all their ducks in a row, the "I have no idea where to begin" couple, the "I just want to keep it simple," the "I just want to have the most memorable, funnest party ever," the "I want to make it jaw dropping," the "I don't want to spend that much (but have really great taste)." I know you.
I've planned your wedding.

LET ME GUIDE YOU

I want to help you. There are a lot of tools out there, and it is often confusing to know where to begin. I want to be able to answer your questions and send you on your way.

Tip: A compelling tale about how you fell in love should guide your decisions.

Let's start this journey together and get you married!

XO
Amina

and
so the
Adventure
begins

01

let's organize a game plan that works for you

There are half a dozen resources out there to get you organized. Let me narrow down your choices.

Tip: You will want a tool that can be shared easily with other helpful planners in your squad, like your future spouse, mothers, best friend, wedding planner, etc.

MY TOP 2 WEDDING ORGANIZING TOOLS

GOOGLE DRIVE

This is the most basic online tool, but it's also the most useful for sharing docs and images amongst your planning squad. You can keep everything private and use excel for things like your guest and vendor list, upload a welcome letter for editing, and/or all your planning files and folders. The only downside to this resource is that you have to categorize the files yourself.

AISLE PLANNER

This online tool is widely used by wedding planners all over the world. It's a great tool for sharing and it's also already organized for you. It literally has everything you could ever need to plan your wedding. It would be hard to shop anywhere else once you have been on here. The only downside to this tool is that you can't connect your Gmail account or your other email accounts to it.

The key here is to find a tool that works best for you and don't waiver. Use the tool of your choice all the way through until your wedding is over! Don't go into this process without picking one! There is a reason there are only two here versus ten. These are the only options you need to choose between. Trust me, I have seen them all.

Pinterest, The Knot, Wedding Wire, Etsy, Instagram...
OMG MY MIND IS GOING TO EXPLODE!

IF YOU DON'T LEARN TO ORGANIZE YOUR FILES, WEDDING PLANNING WILL START TO OVERWHELM YOU.

TIP: Have separate files for cake, personal flowers, ceremony flowers, reception flowers, lighting, bridal gown, bridesmaid dresses, etc. The more breakdowns the better because when you meet with those vendors, you'll have inspiration references at your fingertips. Don't forget to note what you liked about an image so the information is there when it comes time to explain your preferences. For example, if you pinned an inspiration photo of a tabletop, maybe it's the menu you liked and not the flowers, put it in a folder labeled "paper". Be specific and describe what you liked about the menu so you have that information at your paper/invitation meeting.

GO NOW!
MAKE YOUR FILES & FOLDERS.

You don't really need to secure your files with an access-only passcode. If someone really has time to look through your wedding inspirations on platforms like Pinterest, then they have no life. Plus, it's more of a headache for you to invite people to view your private files and make sure they received the invite. Save yourself the time and energy during your wedding planning process.

EXPECTATIONS

EXPECT NOTHING, APPRECIATE EVERYTHING

If we are going to discuss organization, we also need to talk about expectations. It's your wedding, it's okay to have high expectations, high hopes of everything turning out the way you want it to, everyone doing what they are told, and Mother Nature staying in line. My job is not to crush your dreams and it's not to tell you that it can't happen. It CAN be perfect. In fact, it's always perfect – because it's your day!

My job is to give you tips to cope with situations when they don't go as planned, when you go over your budget because you want everything, when your groom doesn't order his suit on time, when one of your bridesmaids doesn't show the enthusiasm you'd hoped for, when your parents are overstepping, when rain shows up in the forecast, or your dress is no longer everything you saw in it nine months ago. These are all scenarios that can put you over the edge. I am here to tell you I am here for you. Let's do this together.

OVER BUDGET

This isn't an unusual concern, and I will give you fast tips on how to tackle budget later. If you aren't an accountant, you are likely to go over your budget. These are just facts. Try to remember that it's only one day – one day where you probably won't notice the extra details you want to purchase, and frankly your guests won't either. Try not to be hard on yourself if you have to cut back. You won't even look back once the wedding is over, but you will if you break your bank. Remember, your wedding decor is not a reflection of your love.

GROOM PROBS

More often than not, your soon-to-be is put on some sort of pedestal because they are also getting married. You're going to assume they are just as excited about "planning" the wedding. I will tell you that most of my grooms who have to go to floral, linen or paper appointments just end up making you mad when you are there, and here is why: They aren't reading or visualizing all the wedding stuff you are, they don't go to weddings and pay attention to what you do and they don't have grand visions of flowers. Cut them some slack, and do yourself a favor, don't give them "jobs" or make them come to meetings where you are setting yourself up for disappointment. Don't ask their opinion if you aren't ready to hear an uninformed answer.

BRIDESMAID STUFF

Here is the deal: There are sometimes one or two bridesmaids, depending on your party, who may be a little fussy. I've experienced the fuss. Often times, it's not even about you. They, in their right minds, would be over the moon happy for you, but sometimes weddings are a reflection of self. Your wedding could be a reflection of their past relationships, or lack thereof, issues with their age and where they envisioned themselves in life. Try with all your might to not take it personally. It's hard to be understanding when it's such a happy time in your life, but they will probably be the life of the party if you don't harp on them too much along the way. Be open to them grieving about their personal life. Trust me, your friendship will go back to normal after the wedding.

When you have doubts in other people during your wedding planning, move on to all the other tasks at hand. There is a lot to plan. It's a happy time, try to find joy in the great moments and keep your eye on the prize.

EXPECTATIONS CONTINUED...

MOTHER NATURE

I've planned a lot of weddings when rain reared its ugly head. The best thing you can do is make a "Plan B", and then on the wedding day, you will feel more at ease that your rain plan was supposed to be a "part of your day." In this case, Plan B becomes Plan A. I had a bride who broke her arm during the reception when she tripped on her dress. Another didn't eat and had to be taken to the hospital after she fainted. This can be avoided (I am only telling you this to remind you to plan to eat before you say your I Do's) if you have a backup plan or eat. Ultimately, go with whatever is forecast for your day, and have a great story to tell your kids or laugh with your friends about over happy hour. Remember you can't control weather!

PARENTS

I am telling you this as a mom of young children: Your parents looked at you when you were four and talked about your wedding day. As you grew up, they think of your boyfriends or girlfriends and wonder if they will be your life partner. Your parents may be divorced, and you may have a complicated dynamic to deal with when planning your wedding. Oftentimes, it can be emotional for them to watch you walk down the aisle because of that little dream they shared when you were four that they are no longer sharing together. Your parents or your mom may be difficult to deal with throughout, but it's important you try to communicate and stay positive. Remember, it's coming from a place of love, and they want to celebrate you.

When you are feeling a little disappointed, try one day of...

CALM BRIDE BINGO

Wake up early	Eat a energizing snack	10 deep breaths	Call a friend	10 wedding pins
Show off your ring	Put "Soon-to-Be-Mrs" on your Starbucks cup	Complete a wedding task	Take a walk	Write down a 2-3 wedding vows
Step away from tech for 10 min.	Stop and smell the roses	FREE SPACE	Sing in the car	Say "HI" to a stranger
Go get your bling cleaned	Be grateful	Put a list together for an emergency wedding day kit	Find places to incorporate cute wedding quotes	Tell someone you appreciate them
Go to bed early	Remind yourself it will get better	Get some fresh air	Look up bride jokes	Sweat for the dress

i love
you
slightly
more
than
prosecco

now that you are all organized...

02

what do you do next? where do you begin?

Some things are more important than others; it just depends on what stage you are in the planning process. I will tell you that the first thing you don't do is set a date because your dream venue may not be available. Don't let this mistake deter your planning.

Let me give you a general monthly checklist, and you can personalize it to what makes sense for you.

MY MONTHLY WEDDING TIMELINE

MONTHS 1 & 2

- Determine your guest list and gather addresses. Remember, guest size is an important factor when it comes to your budget. The bigger your guest list, the more expensive your day will be.
- Discuss budget with the appropriate people, then re-discuss after you book a venue. 50% of your budget goes to venue, food and beverage, and if you go over, you will overspend.
- Tour and secure your venue. Your guest list size will determine your event space size and will affect your estimated food and beverage minimum. If you overestimate your guest list, your minimum quoted at the venue will be higher. It's best to underestimate, within reason.
- Hire your officiant or choose someone to marry you.
- Choose your wedding party in a fun way!
- Hire a DJ/band/ceremony musicians.
- Hire a photographer and/or videographer.
- Book three appointments at different shops for a wedding dress. Remember to cancel the other appointments once you've found "the one."

MONTHS 3 & 4

- Set up your wedding website for guests and include room blocks negotiated with the venue agreement and/or other hotel and restaurant recommendations.
- Book hair and/or makeup consultations and be sure to bring inspiration photos.
- Start gathering inspiration for your wedding design (see previous page on organization of file folders)! Don't be hard on yourself if your wedding look changes over time; this is normal as you get more inspired while planning your day.
- Meet with a paper company or look online to gather inspiration and start picking your favs. Paper is important because it is the first overall feel of what your guests will expect from your wedding design.
- Begin thinking about your ceremony outline and vows.
- Set dates for parties, including engagement, bachelor, bachelorette, shower(s), etc.

MONTHS 5 & 6

- Shop wedding party attire, including attire for the groom!
- Fine tune your wedding design vision and then meet with the florist. Bringing a floor plan or wedding layout to this meeting is helpful. Know who will be getting personal flowers, such as moms, dads, grandparents, aunts, uncles, the officiant, readers, etc.
- Meet with the rental company for linens, chairs, chargers, a tent (including a backup tent), lighting, drapes, lounge furniture, etc.
- Determine your rehearsal dinner location and make sure it is somewhere fun!
- Determine lighting/mood lighting/design lighting.
- Purchase wedding bands.
- Hire any other miscellaneous entertainment and/or babysitting services.
- Give yourself a pat on the back, you're half way done! Don't give yourself a hard time if you are behind!

TIMING IS EVERYTHING.

MONTHS 7 & 8

- Go to your food and beverage tasting. This is your chance to be picky. Make sure you choose foods "most guests" will enjoy. Before this tasting, make requests as to what you really want to taste that's not on the menu and include a vegetarian option to taste or they will pick for you.
- Go to your cake tasting (if the cake is not included in the venue) and make sure you have your design ideas with you or else you will get stuck with what they "always" do. Be specific about what you like because the cake is part of your wedding design.
- Purchase wedding items, such as a cake cutting knife and server, champagne flutes, favors, gifts for each other, parent gifts, wedding party gifts, a guestbook, signage, cocktail napkins, engagement photos or couple photos to display, etc.
- Finalize ceremony/reception music choices.
- Finalize ceremony, rituals, readings, and rehearsal time.
- Start making a must-have photo and family photo list for your photographer.

MONTHS 9 & 10

- Order wedding stationary and mail it eight to ten weeks before your wedding date for out-of-town guests and six to eight weeks for in-town guests (RSVP: 2-3 weeks before your wedding).
- Determine the order for hair and makeup for your wedding party and discuss timing with your hair/makeup vendors.
- Finalize wedding day itinerary with the venue and vendors. Ask your vendors what their schedule looks like and what needs they may have, like meals, tables or power. Final meetings/calls with your vendors are important!
- Purchase wedding attire accessories and bring these items to your fittings to make sure you still like them with your dress. Don't forget to break in your shoes!
- Finalize transportation and your pick-up / drop-off schedule.
- Start preparing any welcome baskets, gifts, and itineraries for those that are traveling.

MONTHS 11 & 12

- Get your marriage license (make sure you look up your requirements/deadline by State).
- Finalize guest seating, food selections/signifiers, escort lists and place cards for assigned seating.
- Print menus and programs, as well as any additional directional signs.
- Have your final dress fittings and make sure your dress gets pressed and put in a protective garment bag.
- Get your ring cleaned professionally by asking ANY jeweler to clean your ring.
- Send your final numbers to the caterer/venue, and include vendor meals (yes, feed your vendors warm meals versus lunch boxes!) Double check your deadline for final counts.
- Place gratuities in envelopes for your vendors and make sure you label the envelopes.
- Do final beauty treatments (don't try out treatments the last month).
- Go through your wedding inventory and label where you want things placed for whomever is helping you decorate.
- GET MARRIED <3 Enjoy your weekend. LOVE LOVE LOVE!

MY VIEW ON THE "FIRST LOOK"

As a wedding planner, I have been a part of many beautiful weddings and I believe there is no single more intimate moment than the first look, that moment when you see your partner before you walk down the aisle. It's a time for the couple to truly be alone and bask in the day with each other, with no one else around them. You will literally not be alone again until you get to your honeymoon suite. During a first look, it's an overwhelming feeling of emotion when you see your partner, and a sense of relief because the getting ready process leads to a lot of anticipation.

What I have experienced is that it doesn't take away from the "walking down the aisle" emotions. The tears, feelings and nerves are all still the same. Every groom has the same emotions as the one that didn't see his bride beforehand. The difference is his head feels clearer because he has seen you in that intimate moment and he can pay attention during the ceremony versus feeling overwhelmed. Every single couple (specifically the groom because it's usually the groom being traditional in not wanting to see the bride) I convinced to do a first look was forever grateful for their decision. On my own wedding day, we did a first look, and I was still nervous during the ceremony. Both my husband and I cried when I walked down the aisle, and both of us felt emotional beforehand, mainly because I made sure we were separated thirty minutes before the ceremony started to be with our girls or guys and gather our thoughts.

Another thing I love about first looks is that you can talk to each other during that time. You don't get to do that when you walk down the aisle, you never discuss how beautiful or handsome either one of you look, and you never get the "full spin" moment in your dress. You only stand there holding hands, saying nothing until your vows. That's what's beautiful about the first look – it's a special time to speak to each other about your day so far and help each other "relax" some.

How about some history? First looks came about because wedding photos have drastically changed. They aren't the "traditional stand up at the altar after the ceremony" photos like we've had before the year 2005. Instead of 20 wedding photos, you take over 1,000. With a first look, before the wedding, you get an incredible forty-five minutes to an hour of picture time together that you will never get after your ceremony when you are stressed and rushing through photos. In fact, if you do a first look before the ceremony, you can minimize photo taking after the ceremony to the wedding party or family only. I like when a couple gets all of their wedding pictures out of the way before the ceremony because they can celebrate and won't feel as much stress after their wedding. Most couples will tell you that taking photos with family and your wedding party is truly the most stressful part of the wedding day. Why not get photos done and head to cocktail hour? Sounds more fun!

DO I NEED A WEDDING PLANNER IF I HAVE THIS GUIDE?

YES & NO...

A wedding planner's job is to keep you on track, but they are also so much more than that. They also help you design your wedding day. They help you find reputable vendors. They negotiate your contracts and tell you what should and shouldn't be included. Wedding planners also give you tips and advice along the way, assist with your wedding day and setting up, make sure the vendors are bringing what they said in their contracts, make well-informed decisions if adjustments have to be made, orchestrate and run the flow of events throughout the day, and some wedding planners even clean up for you at the end of the night.

Some people think friends and family can fill in all the pieces, but most family members are busy getting ready for your wedding day. They are taking photos during important times when a wedding planner would be necessary, or they are having a fun time during your reception (drunk people don't make great helpers either, by the way).

My opinion is to evaluate how much design, referral help, and coordination help you will need along the way, and then hire yourself a day-of coordinator or event manager to come in for the final six to eight weeks to manage the wedding day so you can alleviate a lot of the day-of wedding stress. Evaluate what you need. You might find that you need a wedding planner. You can also decide later and add a wedding planner when you start to feel the heat at any point in your process.

For those of you relying on your venue coordinator, what you need to know is that person only runs the venue – they don't ever see your contracts, know your wedding inspiration or know what's coming onto the property. The onsite person might even have other clients touring (like you did) the day of your wedding so they can see what a wedding setup looks like. Don't be fooled by her title: They are NOT wedding planners. Remember that their main job is to run a smooth operation for the venue first, and you may be one of 50 couples they are working with. The venue coordinator actually prefers wedding planners helping so they can do their job better. They don't want to be bombarded by emails asking questions, phone calls from your parents, or photos of things you are picking out along the way. They want to focus on your venue experience. Trust me, I've done many venue coordinators weddings as their hired wedding planner - the best thing you can do is give them space.

all dressed up... next stop down the aisle.

REAL ADVICE FROM DESIGNER WEDDING GOWN SHOP MARIEE BRIDAL

CARRIE YEO - BRIDAL GOWN & STYLE EXPERT

Most stores will be "made to order" stores, meaning you will not necessarily be able to take your gown off the rack the same day. Typically, gowns you try on are samples. You are then measured once you find your gown to determine your size. Gowns can take anywhere from four to six months to arrive and you will need a further six to eight weeks for alterations. Some stores are off the rack only, and some stores and designers offer a rush fee as an option. This means your gown will be moved to the front of the line and all components and final shipping will be expedited. Make sure you know your wedding date before you start shopping and pick the right type of store for you and your wedding budget.

When choosing who to bring to your appointment, think about who you would take fashion advice from. Your grandma's neighbor may be very sweet, but is she up on the latest trends? Will she have your best interests in mind? Regardless of what you see on TV, most brides only bring three to four guests (this usually includes a mom or stepmom, mother in-law, sisters, and the maid of honor). Once they have purchased the gown, a bride will sometimes bring other people to their fitting before the wedding to make them feel included. A bride who brings a large group can often become stressed while managing family politics and hearing a lot of different opinions. A group of ten guests will not all agree equally on one dress as the clear winner because everyone's taste is different.

When you order your gown, you will usually pay a 50% deposit. You pay the remainder on the delivery of your dress when you have tried it on and checked all the details are correct. It is not usually necessary to pay more than half down unless it is an off-the-rack gown and you are taking it away with you the same day.

DRESS SHOPPING CONTINUED...

Appointments are important and a necessity. It doesn't make sense for a bride to gather her nearest and dearest friends and family and navigate all the way to the bridal store only to arrive and find out there will be a three-hour wait. The appointment will mean that you will know what time to arrive and be seen immediately. Also, remember to cancel your appointment if you cannot make it or if you've already found a dress elsewhere. Not only is this a polite gesture to the store (who will likely have scheduled a member of staff to come in to help you and paid their wage for the two-hour appointment), but it means they can open up the time to another bride. Stores often have waiting lists during the busy season, and although you may feel bad canceling, it is far better than leaving the consultant hanging for two hours.

Bridal sizing is very different than real sizing. It can read several sizes bigger on the label than what you would measure in real life. A bride who is a normal size 6 could easily measure a "bridal" 10 or 12. The consultant will measure your bust, waist and hips.

If in doubt, ask a second consultant to measure you for reassurance.
If you have a small waist and a larger chest, the gown will be ordered in your chest size and then when the gown arrives, it will be big in the waist and need taking in.

Although rare, doubts after you purchase your gown can happen. Once a gown is ordered, it is usually unlikely that it can be cancelled. Go back to the store and try the gown on again. You will likely remember the reasons why you fell in love with it in the first place. If there are still doubts, speak to your consultant about what specific things concern you, as there may be changes that can be made in alterations that will make a huge difference in how you feel.

Tip: Most couples get excited when they begin the wedding planning process, and then it starts to fizzle when life sets in and you fall behind the timeline. Don't fret. Instead, try to play catch up with your wedding checklist because you don't want to be catching up during the last two months before the wedding. It gets busy quickly when RSVPs start arriving.

Staying on track will save you headaches, unnecessary arguments and stress zits!

Try to find a method to remind yourself of your wedding tasks. aisle planner does this by email reminders, but maybe using an online to-do list is helpful like Google Keep or a good old-fashioned day planner!

Let's get you in a wedding state of mind.

what tool will I use to stay on track?

how will I give myself task reminders?

will I hire a wedding planner?

will I have a first look?

who will I bring to my dress appointment?

when is my first dress appointment?

we go
together
like
milk
&
cookies

03

weddings cost lots of money, the end.

Budget is fundamentally one of the hardest things to understand during the wedding planning process, mostly because you don't know what anything costs.

Let me teach you how to navigate wedding spending.

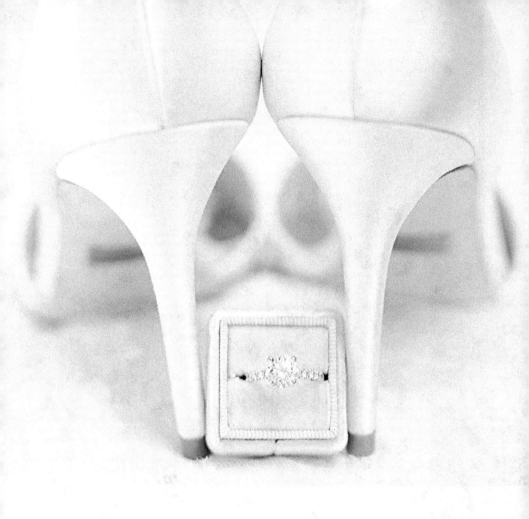

BUDGET
REAL TALK

Do we really have to talk about it, the "b" word, the dreaded "BUDGET"? It's the hardest line item to discuss and manage during your wedding, but you, your partner, and maybe even your parents need to have this conversation before you do any planning, sign any contract, or make any purchases. You shouldn't dream up a wedding you can't financially afford.

It's no fun that way! Build the wedding you can afford from day one and find ways to work with your budget, and then you can have your dream day. If you can get a handle on your budget before your wedding gets out of hand, you will save yourself arguments, tears, and disappointment. Ask yourself: "what is the most important thing I want to experience from my wedding?"

WHO PAYS FOR WHAT?

BRIDE AND/OR BRIDE'S FAMILY

Engagement party
Wedding planner fee
Own travel expenses
Bridal gown, veil, accessories
Bridal hair and makeup
Bridesmaid's hair and makeup (if mandatory)
Wedding stationary, calligraphy, and postage
Groom's wedding ring
Gift for groom
Gifts for bridesmaids
Bridesmaid's bouquets
Pre-wedding parties and bridesmaids luncheon
Photography and videography
Wedding guestbook and other purchases
Total cost of ceremony, including venue, flowers, music, rentals, etc.
Total cost of cocktail hour, dinner and reception, including venue, flowers, music, rental items, lounge furniture, food and beverages, cake, décor, favors, etc.
Transportation for wedding party to ceremony and reception

GROOM AND/OR GROOM'S FAMILY

Own travel expenses and attire
Rehearsal dinner
Wedding gift for the bride
Bride's wedding ring
Gifts for groom's attendants
Bride's bouquet
Father's, Mother's and grandparents' flowers
All boutonnieres
Officiant's fee
Marriage license
Honeymoon expenses

ATTENDANTS

Own attire (including rentals & shoes)
Travel expenses
Bridal shower/bach parties (paid for if they are attending)
Hair and makeup optional (if it's mandatory the Bride pays)

You need some sort of spending guideline. We all do for most things in life, but most especially for your wedding. Vendors will sniff you out if you have an unlimited budget or you don't tell them what you want to spend. You need a starting point, and yes, you can wait for the proposals to come back and work your way back from a dream wedding if need be, but if you say "money is no object," you may not even know what you are really getting. Vendors will just see dollar signs as opposed to, "I am going to make their wedding spectacular." Sorry to disappoint you, but vendors are also running a business.

EST. 100 GUESTS

BUDGET

You may not want to spend 16.2% of your budget on flowers and decor, or 4.8% on stationary. What is important to understand is if you have 10 tables, which is 10 centerpieces, 100 menus, 100 escort cards, 50 invitations (one per couple) and 100 guests to feed and hydrate, your wedding costs will add up. The budget percentage guideline below works for any budget, whether it's $10,000 or $250,000.

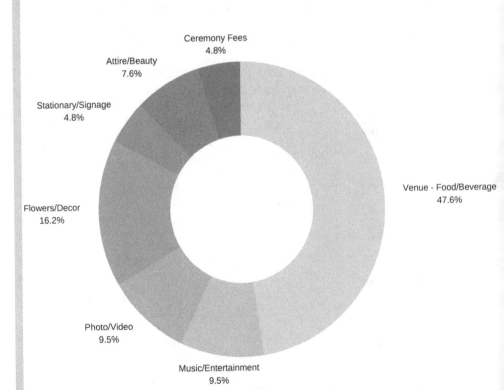

Ceremony Fees
4.8%

Attire/Beauty
7.6%

Stationary/Signage
4.8%

Flowers/Decor
16.2%

Venue - Food/Beverage
47.6%

Photo/Video
9.5%

Music/Entertainment
9.5%

VENDOR COSTS

"YOU GET WHAT YOU PAY FOR."

Nothing is truer than this little saying when it comes to the wedding industry and its vendors.

> "if you think it's expensive to hire a professional, wait until you hire an amateur."
>
> *(Have you heard this yet?!?)*

The above theory does not mean you have to pay for the most expensive vendor, but it does mean that if you fall prey to the lowest price because you are trying to cut corners, you are likely going to be disappointed come wedding day. If you are caught up in disappointment, you will find yourself wishing you took my advice to shop around or negotiate price with a better vendor.

Just because you receive a proposal back doesn't mean the vendor can't work you a better deal. You can always work a better deal or make adjustments that fit your budget. Don't waste your time meeting with another vendor hoping for something drastic to change from one proposal to the next. Speak up and make changes to your proposal, and then decide if you are a good fit for that particular vendor.

WAYS TO LOWER COST

YOU HAVE NOTHING TO LOSE... SO WHY NOT

Venue, food and beverage(s) are 50% of your budget. If you want to save the most money on your wedding budget, you need to negotiate before you sign. If you don't, then you have no "buying power" after you have signed a contract because the venue or caterer already has you locked in to their property or catering contract. Just a heads up, you won't be able to negotiate tax and service fees and you will be alarmed when you see them. However, there are other venue or catering items we can negotiate.

Here are some things you can negotiate ...

- Extra hour of bar if you are buying in a package.
- Upgrade your bar package or no added fees for a specific liquor type (e.g. Grey Goose at no upcharge).
- Extra hors d'oeuvres (1-2).
- Champagne toast included.
- Extra course like soup or palette cleanser included.
- Remove cutting fees if you are bringing in an outside cake to the venue (sometimes it's totally necessary because the pastry chef isn't that great). If you can't get the cake cutting fee removed, see if they could reduce the cake cutting fee.
- Include a dessert or a passed dessert during the reception later into the evening (e.g. smores, cookies and milk, dessert skewers, mini pies, etc.).
- Include a late-night food option (e.g. grilled cheese, French fries, pizza, etc.).
- Honeymoon suite - Usually this is included on your wedding night, so ask for two nights instead of one or an upgraded room. If you get your room for two nights, you can get ready in your suite and have it cleaned "like new" during the ceremony, and then all you have to do is move your groom's belongings over from his room.
- Lower the cost per person for the bar or plated dinner by several dollars (e.g. If your cost pp is $110, ask for $100 pp).
- Waive or reduce the bartender fees.
- Waive or reduce valet fees per car.
- Waive or reduce site or ceremony site fees.
- Negotiate vendor meals before you sign because vendors want hot meals, but a $50 meal for a vendor is pricey.
- Occasionally items like tents, rentals, lighting, even flowers and decor can be added to a venue or catering package. Sometimes (not always), these costs can be drastically inflated where the vendor and the venue or caterer are actually profiting. It would be in your best interest to negotiate or have a cost analysis done by an outside vendor on your own. Make sure the venue or caterer will not charge you for using your own vendors for these items if they package them through the venue, and make sure all of this is written in your contract before you sign.

VENUE AND / OR CATERING

27

WAYS TO LOWER COST

CONTINUED...

Flowers and rentals can add up. I am not talking about rentals for flowers, like containers. I am specifically talking about rentals like table linens and/or napkins, chairs, lounge furniture like sofas, coffee tables, possibly additional lighting, or even a tent if outdoors is your only option and it is starting to look like rain or maybe you are just going for a tented look.

Let's talk about how I can save you some dollars ...

- Pick seasonal flowers and don't limit yourself to only your favorites . If you pick your favorites and they are out of season, not only will they be expensive, but they may be small and not like what you are seeing as you collect inspiration photos.
- Add more greenery or lush greens to fill arrangements and keep in mind that although this can be a good money saver, not all greenery is created equal and some green can drive up costs.
- Buy candles online. Oftentimes it's less expensive than renting and you can send your bridesmaids home with a set of eight for a gift (TIP: Same gift idea goes for napkin rings).
- Four carnations look like one peony and a cabbage rose looks like a peony if peonies aren't in season or out of your price range (they can be quite expensive).
- Don't get too many personal flowers for family; instead of bouquets, get pin-on flowers or corsages for family members.
- Reuse bridesmaid bouquets as decoration for a head table, sweetheart table or around a cake.
- Toss bouquets are usually waived. Don't pay extra if they are not, as this is a negotiable item.
- When you are talking hard goods, you may be able to come down a couple of extra dollars on linens and furniture rentals, or you can ask to reduce the delivery fees.
- Every other table gets a fancy rental linen, or overlay, while the other tables use the house linen (whatever comes with the venue).
- Dress up tables with fancy napkins if you can't afford additional fancy rental linens.
- Do one big grand head table in the middle of the room and spend all of your money here versus the guest tables. You will get a real wow factor as guests walk into the space and save money.
- Most rental companies leave a little room for negotiation, possibly 10-20%, especially if they know you will use them again for future events.
- Try to avoid using lighting from the venue, or any subcontracted rentals, for that matter (these costs are always inflated). Make sure there are no fees prior to signing your venue contract for using outside rental vendors (see previous page).

FLOWERS AND RENTALS

WAYS TO LOWER COST

CONTINUED...

Music and entertainment will make or break your party. There is absolutely no doubt about that. I have had clients say they will use an iPhone and do their own wedding music, and my response is never positive. Whether you have a DJ or band, they are responsible for feeling the crowd and navigating the night and music selections. Don't skimp here, and above all else, please don't hire your fav restaurant DJ or your uncle to be the DJ. They likely have no clue how to MC a wedding, and what you will find is your uncle or whomever will overcompensate for what they don't know. Yikes!

In an effort to save you from an unnecessary party foul, here are ways you can save ...

- Have your DJ or band be your ceremony musicians as well. They can use one speaker and a handheld device for all of your wedding music.
- Don't have a DJ during dinner; this is where an iPhone is actually acceptable. The DJ, or even your venue (if they are doing some sound), can either have another setup if it is a separate location, or just plug in your music to their existing setup and hit play. If you keep their job to a minimum, you may be able to negotiate costs down a little, but don't get too excited because it won't be much. They are still on property, which means they will charge you for the time there. However, if you have live musicians for the ceremony, your DJ or band won't have to start until much later. All you will need to do is negotiate that sound system for your iPhone, and I am sure an on-site coordinator can press play if they won't.
- Negotiate an extra hour of service or waive the other speaker setup fees that may be incurred at each site where they are setting up a sound system.
- Negotiate the lighting package. It's not labor-intensive to have them put up two or three extra lights. If they are charging considerably for a few extras, see if you can get them included in your lighting package.
- Some couples hesitate to hire a band because they really want a DJ. Good news is bands actually take breaks. A band will usually play for forty-five minutes and then take a fifteen minute break (this is normal, but sometimes they play longer). During the breaks, they usually have someone in charge of keeping the party going with your favorite playlist, kind of like a DJ. If you're on the fence with the band because you want a DJ, you shouldn't be because you usually get both, in theory.
- Late night hours are usually after 11PM. If you are getting charged any late-night fees (this goes for any vendors, e.g. florist), waive that cost.

MUSIC / ENTERTAINMENMT

WAYS TO LOWER COST

CONTINUED...

Photographers and videographers are the masters of capturing your day. They gather your family members for all of your important wedding photos and deal with all the people "too excited" to pay attention. They are the storytellers and the ones that will be able to help you relive your day after it's all over. I recommend not finding the least expensive one or least experienced one you can find... it's simply not worth it. Remember you spend your entire day with these people, more than your fiance.

Here are great ways to save on these vendors ...

- I recommend at least eight hours of photography coverage. Anything less and you will miss out on activities like getting ready photos (schedule arrival at the tail-end of makeup completion), cake cutting, or dances, etc. You may have to forgo a "grand exit" photo if you only do eight hours, but that photo may or may not be important to you and honestly, two hours of dancing photos aren't worth the hours when you keep about 3 of those photos. To see more on timeline, check out the sample timeline. With regards to videography, it's the same idea: eight hours, but a lot of clients will average six hours of coverage and get what they need. Keep in mind there simply is not enough time to tell your wedding day story in less than eight hours.
- Be sure at the time of signing you negotiate the cost of extra hours that can be added later (i.e. if you are only buying eight hours of coverage, determine before you sign what it will cost if you need two more hours).
- If you pay for your album later, you can lower your cost. This is my big tip! You might make your own album and be comfortable with that, but make sure you get all your images included with your package versus pay per image. Paying per image will get ridiculous. I would go as far as to say hire a photographer that includes all the images in their package because you can later decide to make whatever albums you want with the images you own. Just make sure, in the contract, your photographer legally allows you to use their images to print.
- Photographers and videographers always have add-ons, so try to get one thrown into your package to incentivize the deal. An add-on may look like an extra album for your parents (although you can also make one online for them if you have all the images). Videographers might throw in a highlight reel or short commercial of your wedding day. The reel is a sweet way to get a glimpse of your big day and totally social media post-worthy.
- Either one of these vendors usually comes with second shooters, and if they do not, I strongly urge you to make sure they do with no additional fees imposed on you. No single person can capture every moment from every angle. It's physically impossible, and you will miss out on many photos or video if you don't have multiple shooters on the ground capturing your day.

PHOTOGRAPHY / VIDEOGRAPHY

all about about wedding flowers.

CARLY CYLINDER - THE FLOWER CHEF

The main piece of information couples don't understand about the cost of wedding flowers is the immense amount of labor involved beyond just delivering beautiful centerpieces. The florist goes to the mart, sources it all, transports it back to the studio, then has to process (unpackage, clean, cut) the flowers, prep the vases, and assemble everything. Then there is more time involved driving and setting up the flowers, and then waiting for the ceremony to end, possibly breaking down or repurposing flowers to another area. Finally, there's sometimes a breakdown where the florists have to come back to your wedding and take it all down. Here are some ways to cut back on design and labor costs.

Focus on color. Many brides want a certain flower like a peony (which has a very short season) or anemone, instead of focusing on color. Allow your florist to use whatever is in season or cheapest that matches the color scheme you love. Color and texture count more than the actual flower used in the grand scheme of design.

Go for greenery. Using a lot of greenery in your wedding will help you save on flower costs. Creating garland down a table looks beautiful and is easy to do. For soft colors, use eucalyptus and olive branches, and for deeper colors, use fern and magnolia.

Start collecting vases ahead of time if you are going to DIY your wedding floral. Ask florists in the area to see if they have leftover vases from a special event they've done that you could buy for cheap or rent. Have your florist use these so they don't have to spend money sourcing them, if your florist doesn't have a large inventory. Make your own centerpieces ahead of time. My best advice is to have the experts make the bouquets for you and then you or someone you assign, or hire, places them for you.

MY BUDGET ESTIMATES

	ESTIMATE	ACTUAL	NOTES
CEREMONY FEES			
VENUE FOOD & BEVERAGE			
MUSIC ENTERTAINMENT			
PHOTOGRAPHY VIDEOGRAPHY			
FLOWERS DECOR			
STATIONARY SIGNAGE			
ATTIRE BEAUTY			
OTHER			

you are my love language

"teamwork makes the dream work"

smooth sailing with the right vendor team

Like anything else, you need to make sure you spend the time assembling the "right" vendor team that understands what your wedding vision is and can help make decisions that best represent what you would want.

I want to help you build your vendor entourage.

04

5 WAYS TO NAIL VENDOR RESEARCH

Read online reviews closely, don't pass judgement on a bad review here or there, and look at consistency. As a vendor with years of experience, out of 180 reviews, I had 4.9 stars. I had a couple of clients that were awful to work with, and this happens to other vendors, too, so really spend time finding consistent feedback and know every couple writing the reviews may not be a peach.

Look at their social media. Do you connect with what you see and how they communicate to their audience? Do they sound and look professional? Funny is cute, but serious is better.

Ask the venue, but do your research after they hand you their vendor list. It's usually their list of buddies who they like to work with. This doesn't mean they aren't great, as most of them could be, but it doesn't mean they are ALL great.

Ask your hired vendors for referrals, but do your research. The same goes for their vendor list similar to that of the venue's list. It doesn't mean they are a fit for you or all that great.

Meet in person and view their work! Ask yourself, do you trust them? Do you connect with their work? Are they serious about what they do? You aren't becoming friends; it's about the work they will provide you on your wedding day. No matter how much you love them, remember that you are paying them to provide a service. Some of the sweetest vendors I have worked with are the worst vendors when it comes to turn around time or responsiveness. Friendship with your vendor should only be a bonus to this hiring relationship.

FIND THE RIGHT VENDORS

It's important to spend the time doing your wedding research and not just pick your first vendor solely based on the website you connect with the most. Here is why: Most high school graduates can make a swanky website, but do you want a 19-year-old with no wedding experience in charge of the most important day of your life?

My Wedding
Vendor Entourage

VENDOR NOTES

COMPANY NAME:
_____

VENDOR TYPE: PHONE:
_____   _____

CONTACT: EMAIL:
_____   _____

FAV THINGS I LIKE ABOUT
THIS VENDOR

QUESTIONS TO ASK WHEN VISITING A
VENUE

1. Will there be other events on the premises the same day, and if so, how close will those events be to mine? Will we have to share the ceremony location with other couples, putting us in a certain time frame?

2. What time are vendors allowed to set-up? Can we store rentals overnight for pickup the following morning? Or do we need to be out that evening?

3. How late can the music play? What are the outside noise restrictions?

4. What is the maximum amount of hours we can have the space? Are there overtime fees?

5. Are there parking facilities? Do you have valet available? Overflow parking? Overnight parking? Any restrictions for transportation companies or drop-offs?

6. Where can the bride and groom get ready on wedding day? What time are getting ready rooms available to us? Are we allowed to bring in outside food or drinks?

7. If there is rain, how does the venue accommodate the ceremony and reception if they are outdoors? Are there extra fees incurred on our end?

8. Are there any limitations to décor, candles, fireworks, confetti, sound, etc.?

9. Do you require insurance from us? Vendor insurance?

10. Where are the restrooms located?

11. What is the waitstaff-to-guest ratio?

12. After we have booked the facility, will there be an opportunity for food tastings? Tell me about that experience.

13. Can you show me layouts in the spaces I am looking at that will accommodate my estimated guest size (remember NOT to overestimate or drastically underestimate)?

14. Can you send me an estimate after this walk-through including food and beverage, champagne toast, cake cutting, vendor charges and/or any additional service fees you may charge on your banquet orders? (You'll want to see this estimate before you sign contract and see my note in #13 regarding guest size estimate.)

15. Do you provide a honeymoon suite for the night? When can I get into this room?

16. Tell me about the amenities your property has that we can utilize on the wedding day.

QUESTIONS TO ASK WHEN INTERVIEWING A
OFFICIANT

1. What are your fees?

2. Do you adhere to a particular ceremony script?

3. What kind of personal touches can we make to the ceremony script?

4. Do you impose any restrictions with photography? Videography? Music? Décor?

5. Can you be present at rehearsal and assist in conducting it? If so, is there an additional fee? (This is not necessary if you have someone directing your rehearsal.)

6. Are we allowed to write our own wedding vows? Can you help guide this process?

7. Are there restrictions on the types of readings that can be used?

8. How many weddings do you schedule the same day? How do we assure you get to us on time?

9. What do you wear?

10. When would we be able to see a copy of our written ceremony?

11. Do you come with your own microphone and speaker, or will one need to be provided?

12. Will you assist us in guiding the timing of the ceremony for the wedding day, including when we would sign our marriage license and recommendations on who would sign with us? (I personally recommend family versus friends as witnesses, (if you need them) because family is forever.

13. What are your fees? What is your payment policy? Cancellation policy? Do you have a contract or agreement letter we can sign to assure your presence? What is your back-up plan if you get sick or have car trouble?

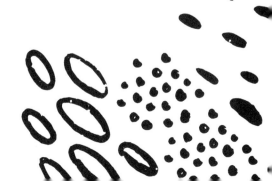

DJ/BAND

1. What will you wear on wedding day?

2. Have you worked at the venue before? If not, what set-up requirements do you have? Power requirements? Storage for equipment?

3. How large are your speakers? Where will the speakers be set during the ceremony, and can they be hidden if they are robust so we can avoid seeing them in photos?

4. What type of lighting do you have included and what are the colors? What other effects during your performance do you use that I need to be aware of (or opt out of)?

5. What type of entertainer are you? Do you just make announcements, or are you narrating the entire time we are cutting our cake or during our first dance? Tip: I never prefer a MC who talks a lot because it forces your guests to listen to what the MC is saying the entire time versus enjoying the moments.

6. If you aren't the MC or DJ during the event, am I able to speak with this person directly when I discuss my wants and needs?

7. How many hours will you play? Are there overtime fees? What do your breaks look like (band)?

8. Can I get recommended song lists from you? How involved are you with helping us choose music?

9. How do you handle requests at the reception if I do not want requests?

10. Do you play any songs or special activities to get the crowd involved? Tip: Try not to break up your dinner or reception with a lot of activities, as it'll starts to feel like a circus e.g. shoe game (not a fan)

11. Do you provide microphones for the ceremony? Music for the ceremony? Cocktail hour? Dinner?

12. Do you need a meal during the reception? How many?

13. What are your fees? What is your payment policy? Cancellation policy? Do you have a contract or agreement letter we can sign to assure your presence? What is your back-up plan if you get sick or have car trouble?

QUESTIONS TO ASK WHEN INTERVIEWING A

PHOTOGRAPHER/VIDEOGRAPHER

1. What are your favorite moments to capture?

2. What do you consider your style to most be like?

3. What kind of equipment do you usually bring?

4. How many weddings have you shot?

5. What is your experience at the venue? If none, when will you tour the property to decide where to capture photos?

6. Are we able to own all of the digital images after the event is over? (photographer) Who keeps the raw footage? (videography)

7. How long does it take to get a sneak peak of what you captured? When are the photos/video delivered in full?

8. Do you come with back-up equipment? How many cameras do you bring to the job? How are you protecting the images/footage throughout the day?

9. How many people are onsite with you? Tip: You must have a second shooter because one shooter can't capture every moment (as mentioned previously).

10. Do you design your own albums? Can I work with you on the design? (photography) How do you decide what footage makes it and what doesn't? (videography)

11. When do you usually arrive the day of the event? Do you stay the entire time? What is your extra hourly rate? Tip: You need a minimum of seven to eight hours for both photo and video (as mentioned previously).

12. Do you edit every picture you take? (photography)

13. How many photos do you take at an average wedding? (photography) How much footage do you get on wedding day? (videography)

14. What are your fees? What is your payment policy? Cancellation policy? Do you have a contract or agreement letter we can sign to assure your presence? What is your back-up plan if you get sick or have car trouble?

suddenly
all the
love
songs
were
about
you

0
5

good design begins with an even better story

Designing a wedding was always my favorite part of the planning process because I paid specific attention to what made my couple unique. Ask yourself, what makes you two unique? What do people love about you together? How will you bring these elements out in your wedding design?

Let's learn some basic design ideas you can take with you while you plan.

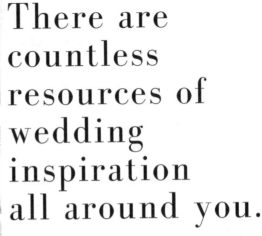

There are countless resources of wedding inspiration all around you.

where will you get your wedding inspiration?

Don't limit yourself to only wedding inspiration you find online or in bridal magazines. Open your eyes to home design, restaurant looks, fashion trends, and window displays. Ask yourself, what am I drawn to? You will be amazed by the inspiration you can find all around you when you start to open your eyes and begin incorporating these unique ideas into your wedding design.

Remember, make sure what you are incorporating is unique to you and your fiance, or there will be a disconnect to the overall feeling of your wedding. For instance, if you aren't into the outdoors, you shouldn't have a farm-inspired wedding. If your wedding is really feminine, and your partner isn't in touch with his feminine side of all the pinks and purples you are choosing, you should consider dialing back the elements that don't unite you two at "your wedding". Do you get where I am going here?

COLORS

What color will you choose? Here are the most popular choices over the years (other than whites and metallics).

black

lavender

light pink

navy

baby blue

scarlet red

kelly green

peach

Sometimes choosing your wedding palette is the hardest part of the design process. Pick something that speaks to you, not just a color that is "trending". We all know the trend will die and you will be stuck with your wedding colors forever.

Make sure to include one neutral color or a base color so you have something to work with. Neutrals in the families of black, brown, white (includes off-white, eggshell, ivory) metallics like gold, rose gold, silver, bronze, champagne, etc. are all great options.

Consider these details when choosing a wedding color: the time of year or season, your venue (will your colors clash or will your venue feel united with your color/design scheme?), your wedding "theme," formality of your event, will the colors fit you both or will it feel like only an extension of one of you, etc.

Head to Home Depot, or any home improvement store, and hit the paint aisle. Play around with paint swatches and have some fun in the family of colors you two are drawn to. Keep the swatches for all your design meetings.

INSPIRATION

There are four color combinations and looks that I believe will stand the test of time. These are what I consider the classics and safe bets.

BLACK & WHITE

BLUSH & CREAM

RED & METALLIC

BROWN & NATURAL

If you are having a tough time deciding what color combo or look to go with, there are fun color pickers online to give you a good starting place; just Google "wedding color picker." You can always do a couple inspiration boards and start collecting what you are drawn to. You will see the more you collect, the more you will define your look and your final wedding design and direction.

Feel safe in knowing that once you visit the florist and start discussing design, they will help you through roadblocks. You can always request a sample from the florist as well, and they can deliver it at your food tasting or you can visit their shop and play around with the look with them. If you want to add more of a certain color or change something up, it's a great time to do it and evolve your look into your final masterpiece!

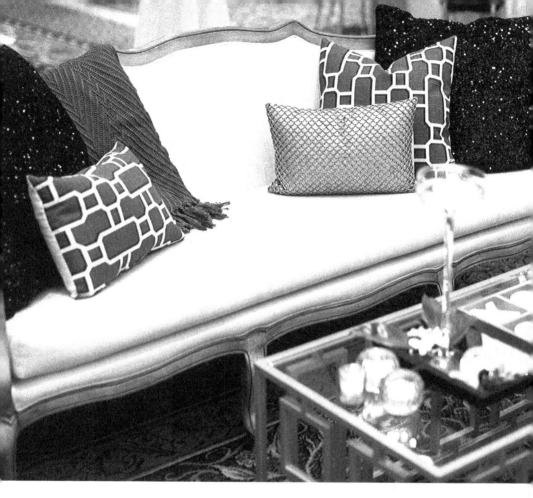

LAYERS
DESIGN SPEAK

Layers have become a huge part of weddings. Combining layers can help you achieve a harmonious composition. It's beyond putting an overlay on a polyester cotton linen table cloth. It's about creating wedding dimension, unity in your look, introducing patterns, shapes, and building a sense of scale. Adding layers doesn't just mean adding a different color; it can mean adding a new texture, a new fiber, or a different shape throughout your entire wedding.

Don't be afraid of adding layers to create a sophisticated setting, or to create vibrant talking points throughout your wedding weekend. Maybe you have three table linens in the same color, but all in a different fiber or texture. Maybe you include several layers and textures in your floral design, but all in white to create more of a classic look. Maybe you vary the same pattern in different scales or sizes from paper to floral to linen throughout your entire design.

Love you
more.
the end.
i win.

06

compile all the details in one place

Your wedding day timing is your "wedding bible" and everyone involved in your wedding needs to be on the same page.

As an experienced wedding planner, I created a timeline with a great flow from event to event. Lucky for you, I have made you a sample.

THE FINAL COUNTDOWN
WHEELS GO ROUND AND ROUND

Your RSVPs have started coming in and you must make calls to those who haven't mailed in cards, as well as calls to those who have mailed in cards but have included a name on the card of someone that was not invited. You have to start assigning your guests to tables and start tallying up food counts. Dress fittings are happening, family is calling and bridesmaids want information. Vendors are also emailing and wanting all the day-of details and your final selections.

This isn't even to mention that it's setting in that you are about to get married. It's important to take a moment to build a separate, short to-do list of wedding tasks, and possibly even give some of your friends and family a short list of wedding tasks, too. There are probably family members or friends waiting on the sidelines waiting for this moment. Don't let all of these wedding tasks start to bring on stress. Let's tackle this head on together. You've got this!

MY WEDDING
TASK LIST

MY TO-DO LIST

WHO CAN HELP ME?

URGENT WEDDING TASKS

SEATING

When your RSVPs start coming in two to three weeks before your wedding, you need to get down to business, and it can be quite complicated if you don't start thinking about it before they arrive. You should have a general idea of the definite 'yes' guests, and you can start grouping them according to how you know them. Also consider getting your parents involved when it comes to their friends, this will help!

ESCORT CARDS

A lot of couples think they have to assign every seat, but you do not! Assigning a table is the easiest method. Oftentimes, the guest will put a pre-selected food choice on an RSVP, and you will then put their food choice on their escort card in the form of a signifier. The signifier can be a shape like a cow, fish, or chicken, a rhinestone, or a different color escort card. The escort cards will go in alphabetical order (by last name) on a table outside of the dining room. The guests will take their cards to the table and place it in front of their setting, and the service staff will know what they ordered. Simple!

PLACE CARDS

Place cards are meant for when you want to assign seats. They are already at the place setting when the guest arrives to the table. This is more daunting if you plan to do this for the entire group, as assigning them a table is hard enough. This is the most formal way of seating your guests. I will, however, recommend to my client to always assign their head table if they have one, as well as their parent's tables. This is because parents and the wedding party sit last. It's best they know exactly where to go rather than shuffle around, plus your parents want a good seat so they can see you during dinner and while toasts are occurring.

SEATING CHARTS

Seating chalkboards, seating mirrors, seating boards: These are similar in theory to an escort card. These are put up letting guests know what table to sit at. You may already have a place card sitting at the table when they arrive, or you may just let them choose where to sit in the case of a buffet or tableside dinner service where the guests can choose what meal they want when they arrive to the table (not mailed in), or family-style service where food is set on the table and shared. These boards/mirrors/signs are also alphabetized by last name.

VENUE CHECKLIST

Along with the vendors and all those involved in your wedding needing to know details about your wedding day timeline, your venue needs details, too. Put all the below information in one spreadsheet, word doc, or email so they can prepare their banquet orders.

01 Vendors

They are going to want to know who your vendors are, what their contact info is, when they will arrive and what they need to provide them e.g. DJ table for ceremony, cocktail hour, reception? Staging for band? Break room?

02 Ceremony

How many chairs are needed? Water station? Gift table? Ceremony table? Linens? LAV or microphone for groom and officiant? Do musicians need chairs?

03 Cocktail Hour

How many high and low tables with chairs? Linens? Bars? Water station? Gift table? Guestbook table? Cocktail Napkins? Votives? Musician chairs? DJ table? Lighting?

04 Dinner/Reception

Head table or sweetheart table for the bride and groom? How many guest tables? Chair counts at each table? High chairs? VIP tables? Cake table? Misc. tables? Linens? Napkins? Napkin fold? Menus? Dance floor size? Entertainment needs? Power needs? Votives? Chargers? Specialty china? Specialty glassware? Specialty flatware?

05 Food Counts

Adults, # Children 12 and Under, # 21 and under, # Vendor Meals, Special needs? Food restrictions? Food signifiers (read about this on the previous page under "escort cards")?

The venue doesn't normally need final counts except for a few days before your event, but read your contract to be sure

SAMPLE CHURCH WEDDING DAY

8:00AM	Bride & bridesmaids arrive to bridal suite
8:30AM	Hair/makeup artists arrive
8:45AM	Jenny hair, Katie makeup
9:30AM	Katie hair, Jenny makeup
10:15AM	Bridal hair, Lizzy makeup (FG)
11:15AM	Bridal makeup, Lizzy hair (FG)
11:30AM	Photographer/videographer arrives
11:30AM	Groom & groomsmen begin getting ready
12:15PM	Bride gets in dress (allow for 30 minutes)
1:00PM	Wedding party leaves hotel for church
2:00PM	Guests begin arriving, wedding party hidden
2:30PM	Ceremony begins
3:30PM	Photos at church - make a photography shot list
4:30PM	Transportation leaves for venue
5:00PM	Cocktail hour
5:00PM	Additional wedding party photos
5:15PM	Couple photos (you get more pics if you do a first look!)
5:50PM	Couple views reception room for the first time
6:00PM	Guests invited to dinner
6:15PM	Grand entry (with or without wedding party)
6:20PM	First dance
6:25PM	Father daughter/Mother son dance-2.5 min ea.
6:30PM	First course
7:00PM	Main course
7:20PM	Toasts begin - best man, maid of honor, dad
7:35PM	Dance floor opens
8:00PM	Cake cutting
8:20PM	Bouquet/garter toss
8:30PM	Photographer/videographer ends (9 Hours)
10:00PM	Late night food served
11:00PM	Reception ends/grand exit optional

SAMPLE HOTEL/VENUE WEDDING DAY

10:30AM	Bride & bridesmaids arrive to bridal suite
10:45AM	Hair/makeup artists arrive
11:00AM	Jenny hair, Katie makeup
11:45AM	Katie hair, Jenny makeup
12:30PM	Bridal hair, Lizzy makeup (FG)
1:30PM	Groom & groomsmen begin getting ready
1:30PM	Bridal makeup, Lizzy hair (FG)
1:45PM	Photographer/videographer arrives
2:30PM	Bride gets in dress (allow for 30 minutes)
3:00PM	First look followed by couple photos
4:00PM	Wedding party photos
4:30PM	Family photos - make a photography shot list
5:00PM	Guests begin arriving, wedding party hidden
5:30PM	Ceremony begins
6:00PM	Cocktail hour
6:50PM	Couple views reception room for the first time
7:00PM	Guests are invited to dinner
7:15PM	Grand entry (with or without wedding party)
7:20PM	First dance
7:25PM	Father daughter/Mother son dance-2.5 min ea.
7:30PM	First course
8:00PM	Main course
8:20PM	Toasts begin - best man, maid of honor, dad
8:35PM	Dance floor opens
9:15PM	Cake cutting
9:30PM	Bouquet/garter toss
9:45PM	Photographer/videographer ends (8 Hours)
10:30PM	Late night food served
11:30PM	Reception ends/grand exit optional

you
are my
today
and
all of
my
tomorrows

07

she lived happily ever after.

APPENDIX

Just a few extra goodies from me to you.

LINGO

abbreviations you might hear...

AV	Audio Visual - equipment for sound & visual
B2B	Bride-to-be
BEO	Banquet Event Order
BM	Bridesmaid or Best Man
BOUT	Boutonniere (pin on flower)
CHARGER	Decorative plate underneath dining plate
CONSUMPTION	Paying for only what is consumed
CONTINGENCY	Back-up plan for weather
F&B MINIMUM	Min. amount you have to spend on food and beverage
FG	Flower Girl
FOB	Father of the Bride
FOG	Father of the Groom
GM	Groomsmen
IN-HOUSE	Available to use at the venue: like linens, chairs, china
LAV	Microphone attached to clothing for groom or officiant
LED	Light source that uses very little electricity
LINEN	Table cloth
LOAD-IN	Location to bring items in for the event
MC	Master of Ceremonies, the announcer at your event (DJ)
MOB	Mother of the Bride
MOH	Maid of Honor
PLUS PLUS (++)	Not Included in the price (tax, service, gratuities)
RACK RATE	Suggested retail price (hotel rooms)
SET	Your event setup or event time
STD	Save-the-Date
STRIKE	Clean-up

Don't worry, no one expects you to know the LINGO, but it's good to pretend you do when negotiating because it makes you sound like you understand how events work. This makes you a valuable client.

MY WEDDING NOTES

○

DAYS UNTIL MY WEDDING

IMPORTANT NOTE

TAKE AWAY TIPS FOR
YOUR CEREMONY

- I prefer no guestbook at a ceremony because it holds up the seating process and most people will run "on time." If they are "on time," your entire event will run late if guests have to sign a guestbook before they sit for the ceremony. As an option, introduce the guestbook at cocktail hour.

- There should be one usher per fifty guests. Ushers traditionally usher in a church, so you don't need ushers at a venue, but I recommend them as helpers or greeters at the ceremony. They can help get people seated in groups of four or more if guests aren't sitting when they arrive. The ushers or helpers can also balance the ceremony seating for each side of the aisle so they look even for photo reasons.

- Programs have information about those included in your wedding party or on the service like music or readers. Programs can be used, and should be the ONLY place you use, an "In Memory of." I don't recommend memory tables or empty chairs in the front row of your ceremony for photo reasons as well.

- Order of Procession: Grandparents of the bride, grandparents of the groom, parents of the groom, mother of the bride, wedding party, maid of honor/best man, the kiddos, and last, the bride. Alternatively, all the guys can walk up with the groom down the aisle before the procession begins, or in through the side before the processional begins, or after mother of the bride walks down the aisle (but before the bridesmaids).

- It's okay to walk down the aisle alone if there are two dads, and it's ok to walk with both, or with one dad at the beginning of the aisle and the other dad jumping in closer to the end.

- If there is tension between any divorced parents, dad and his date/spouse/girlfriend can sit in the second row and Mom and hers sit in the first row. Mom always gets the first seat in the first row, on either side. It's called "the seat of honor," and most moms love this idea when you tell them.

- Jr. bridesmaids/Jr. groomsmen – 10-14 years old; ring bearers/flower girls 3-7 years old (I recommend one parent at the front of the aisle and one parent at the back of the aisle to assist in getting the littles down the aisle). For the youngest wedding party members, they will usually sit during the ceremony with their parents or grandparents, and it's easier to have them NOT walk in the recessional.

- If there is a pet, have a designated person to look after them during the ceremony after they "walk" down the aisle. Alternatively, if you are done with wedding photos with your four-legged friend, then have someone take them home, or back with them to look after them while you are gone.

- Heels in the grass: Walk on your toes! Heels on any steps: Feel out the staircase when you walk down the steps and try not to look down. You can do it!

- The maid of honor (or person closest to the bride) will hold the bride's bouquet during the ceremony. She will hand off her bouquet to the next bridesmaid in line, and then grab it back after she fixes the bride's dress right after the bride gives her dad a hug and the groom shakes the dad's hand. Make sure you stand close to your Groom!

- No receiving lines if you have over 100 guests. If you do have one, you don't have to greet guests again later during the reception, but receiving lines are meant for churches. Honestly, no one really likes standing in line waiting to give an awkward "Congratulations." It's a weird way to start a cocktail hour or a dinner reception, but if you choose to have a receiving line, have one outside the church. Otherwise, make your rounds during the dinner in between each meal course, that way you can eat and greet the guests.

TAKE AWAY TIPS FOR
YOUR COCKTAIL HOUR

- If you have a monogram, it can be used for the first time with the new initial at cocktail hour. It shouldn't be on any paper pre-ceremony, not even an invitation.

- Make sure you have some tall cocktail tables and low cocktail tables with seating for your older guests. Cocktail hour is also a great place to introduce some lounge furniture if you have it in your budget. Sometimes venues will have furniture that you can move to cocktail hour or your reception.

- The bride and groom can attend cocktail hour without any formal announcement after photos.

- No tip jars for bartenders should EVER be allowed and please make sure you request this. It's very tacky to invite people to your wedding and have a tip jar. You should cover your bartender tips. Cash bars aren't my favorite option either. Set a budget for your bar with the caterer or venue, and once you get close to reaching that budget amount or limit, go to a cash bar if you must. Alternatively, serve only beer, wine and a signature drink to save money.

- There should be one bartender per seventy-five guests. Don't cut corners here because bar lines are no fun. If your venue allows, have "bartender relief" with wine, beer or signature drink passed or on a station where guests can serve themselves as needed.

- Your cocktail hour shouldn't exceed one hour. Between us, forty-five minutes is actually a perfect cocktail time-frame.

- If you are going to serve booze, you will need some sort of food at cocktail hour. Don't skimp on food or you will have "hangry" and possibly drunk guests.

- In the same thought, don't over serve your guests cocktail hour food. Your guests will get too full to enjoy their meal, or overeat at dinner and then not have the energy to dance all night long.

- When you are picking cocktail hour food, consider at least one station. It could be a cheese and fruit station if you are on a budget. Stations are a great way to get guests fed quickly without them having to wait for passed food. Although, passed food is a great option as well, this way guests don't have to leave their great conversations adding to their fun experience.

- Also, keep in mind that your guests have 2 hands, one for a drink and one for food. Try not to pick food that they need a utensil for. Although it's cute, if your cocktail hour requires a place for every guests to put their drink down in order to each your cocktail hour food, this might take away from your guest's experience.

- Don't forget to include music. Something to set the tone of what is yet to come. Something more upbeat than your ceremony.

- You certainly can also add some sort of "game" or activity to your cocktail hour, but keep in mind that most guests are chatting for the first time with each other. They may want to catch up, or just enjoy their food and drink. Don't rack your brain thinking of cocktail hour activities, most likely your guests won't partake.

- Signature drinks are an awesome detail, but don't make them so crafty that it takes your bartender 4 minutes to make each drink. This will hold up the bar line. Sometimes the bartenders can pre-make your signature drink and this will help move your bar lines.

- Your cocktail hour is the perfect time to introduce a guestbook, but don't put it at the entry to your cocktail hour, as it will hold people up walking in, similar to that of the ceremony.

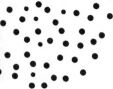

TAKE AWAY TIPS FOR YOUR DINNER

- Typically, only the host parents will toast to the couple versus the ones NOT paying for the dinner. I recommend only the hosts, maid of honor or a representative from the bride's side, and best man or representative from the groom's side to toast. Pick the funniest person to toast last. A great time for the couple to do a toast is after the cake cutting or even at the start of the dinner. Try to give toasters a time-limit (except for the parent hosts). A great toast is no longer than five minutes.

- Make sure parents have the best seats during dinner and their table is located where they can see the couple as well. Use place cards for parent tables to reserve their seat.

- You don't need to do a grand entry if the dinner is separate from the dancing space. Instead, it can be during the dancing portion of the reception when guests move from dinner to dancing locations. If it's in the same space, plan for your grand entry fifteen minutes after guests are invited to sit for dinner, as this will get them in the room. The wedding party should be told prior to reception to wait outside the room with the couple if they are getting announced as well.

- Don't make the guests wait thru toasts and dancing before food is served - "hangry."

- Make sure to continue with the fun music throughout dinner. Dinner music shouldn't be an afterthought.

- Wine service during dinner is a great way to cut back on bar costs if your venue allows you to pause the bar. You don't have to offer more than 2 options - white and red. Often times the house wine will suffice. You can pick a nicer wine for your parents and head table if you want to get more specific.

- The Bride and Groom can have their own special dinner if there is something memorable that you want for dinner.

- Buffets are still great options, however, have the venue or caterer be more creative with what they are serving food in and don't neglect decor on your buffet tables.

- When releasing buffet tables, have your DJ release a few tables at a time, this will avoid long lines. The DJ can make the announcement to stay seated until their table is released. This helps regulate buffet lines and your guest experience.

- If you want to serve cake at dinner, cut the cake as the salad course is served so people can see your cake before it's cut. You can do this by putting the cake at the dinner space entry as guests walk in so they can view it before they sit.

- Try to avoid dinner interruptions like "the shoe game." DJs tend to love this game, I am certain it was created by a cheesy wedding DJ from 1980.

- Visit the guests during each course change and say, "Thank you for coming." Don't forget to go back and eat because the service staff is usually waiting on you to sit back down to service dinner.

TAKE AWAY TIPS FOR YOUR PARTY

- Grand entries sometimes will include parents and flower girls or ring bearers, but it is not as common.

- Cake cutting: Traditionally, the groom's hand lays over the bride's hand, and they cut a corner of the bottom layer. This should be a piece big enough for two bites. The bride gets fed first, then the groom, and then a long kiss post cutting so your photographer can get a great photo. After the cake cutting is also a great time for the newlyweds to make a toast if you didn't do so at dinner!

- Serve parents cake first, and then your guests.

- The optional groom's cake can be rolled out as a surprise and cut after the main cake is cut.

- Guests are allowed to leave after the cake cutting. Don't be alarmed if this happens, as it's normal.

- You don't have to do a garter toss or a bouquet toss if you don't want to; or you can do one and not the other.

- Avoid dollar dances or anything asking for money unless it's a family tradition - your family expects this - if it's not, it seems odd because most people don't carry cash to a wedding.

- Leave your wedding on a high note! Don't let there be five people left in the room, unless you envision it being this way, you can always cut your DJ off early if your party starts to die. It's always nice to go out with a bang rather than a fizzle. You can always move the party to the nearest bar or someone's hotel room or house to continue the fun.

- Late night food is a really great way to keep the party going. It soaks up the alcohol and gives your guests an energy boost. I have had couples want to incorporate a food truck as late night food. This involves moving people away from the dance floor and outside. If your guests go outside, they are less likely to return to the dance floor if it's too far. Keep your party going strong and consider having late night food closer to the party.

- When you are picking music, it's important to ask yourselves the question, "what will your guests enjoy?" This includes grandma, grandpa, and everyone over the age of 45. I always say, a good rule of thumb is to play a variety of music, especially music guests will dance to right after dinner. Then, as your party continues and most of the older people leave, you can kick it up a notch or start to incorporate your specific music. This keeps your party memorable as opposed to "not that fun".

- The Bride and Groom, the Wedding Party, and the Parents need to all be in charge of getting people to the dance floor and having a fun experience. Make them aware of this before wedding day so they know it's important to you that all of the guests have a great time if they start to see a slow dance floor.

- If there is music you absolutely do NOT want to hear. Make sure your DJ knows what that is. If you don't want them taking requests make sure they know this too!
-
- Getaways are great, but often times unnecessary or a waste of money. You can slip out or leave with the guests and this is totally acceptable and oftentimes easier to orchestrate then wrangling drunk people all at the same time.

- Have a blast, and don't get too intoxicated. You don't want your wedding to become bad gossip or feel like you don't remember parts of it.

Advice From Experience

"Details are fun, but don't forget what actually matters. The day is about committing to each other as husband and wife."-- Whitney Lewis, Owner of Some Like It Classic, award winning Wedding Design company, Phoenix, AZ

"When choosing a wedding dress, I always advise comfort over style. If you feel uncomfortable your entire day, you will look uncomfortable." -- Rupa Vora, Owner of Studio East, award-winning dress design shop, Chicago, IL

"If I was going to put on a big wedding I wanted to make sure that everyone could look back at the day and feel special. People will always remember how they were treated and my wedding was no exception." -- Morgan Cooper, daughter-in-law of Rock Legend Alice Cooper

"I acted like my wedding was a month earlier in hopes that I would have time to "relax" a bit the last month. I would do it again the same way because everything adds up more than you anticipate." -- Kaile Kyle, wife of Superbowl Champ Jason Kyle

FINAL WORDS FROM YOURS TRULY

XO
Amina

Enjoy this entire wonderful, exciting process. It is the ONLY TIME in your life this will happen for you with this person. Remember to be kind to your parents who are involved and that little story I shared with you earlier. They are just as overwhelmed and excited for you and want everything to be total perfection. On your wedding weekend, carve out a little alone time for you and your partner to grab a coffee, have breakfast, go on a hike or bike ride to just reflect on your weekend before your friends and family take over. On your wedding day, make time for yourself too, buy a journal for you and your partner that you write in and exchange on the wedding day and take twenty minutes to reflect on what you are feeling, or take an extra-long shower, sit for a few minutes and just breathe. You may do a lot of "just breathing" throughout the planning, and that's okay. It's good for you!

Don't drink too much, especially before your ceremony. You want to remember your wedding and the entire event. In fact, drink lots of water and eat a hearty breakfast and lunch! By nature, I like to have fun, too, but this is an expensive and important event for you. You want to be present, especially after you took all this time to plan and stress.

Lastly, the day goes by incredibly fast. Find joy in every corner, even in the mistakes or whatever crazy thing that pops up. Have a beautiful wedding. I am truly so happy I could be a part of it, and hopefully some of my advice was successful for you! If it was, I would love to hear about it! If you are still planning and you have additional questions, I am here for you.

THE
END

DISCLAIMER

The information provided in this book is designed to provide helpful information on helpful topics related to weddings and wedding planning. The information in this book is true and complete to the best of our knowledge. All recommendations are made without guarantee on part of the author, publishing or printing companies. All those involved, including the author, disclaim any liability in connection with the use of this information. It is best to read all your legal contracts before you sign, as you assume sole responsibility. The author or bridecollective.co in no event shall be liable for any special, direct, indirect, consequential, or incidental damages or any damages whatsoever, where in an action of contract, negligence or arising out of or in connection with the use of the information found in this book.

Made in USA - Kendallville, IN
1036119_9781703336870
12 16 2019 0950